A GUIDE TO
EVERGLADES
NATIONAL PARK
AND THE NEARBY
FLORIDA KEYS

by HERBERT S. ZIM, Ph.D., Sc.D.
with the cooperation of
Florida National Parks and Monuments Association, Inc.
(Formerly the Everglades Natural History Association)

illustrated by Russ Smiley

Golden Books® • **NEW YORK**

Distributed by:
Florida National Parks and Monuments Association, Inc.
Homestead, FL 33030 Phone: (305) 247-1216

FOREWORD

As the title suggests, this book was originally designed to serve as a guide to Everglades National Park and the southernmost region of the state. To insure that this classic publication remains a viable guide for the south Florida visitor, it has been updated to include information on Biscayne National Park and the Big Cypress National Preserve, both established since the initial publication date in 1960. This guide has been prepared in collaboration with the Florida National Parks and Monuments Association, Inc., to assist you in enjoying your National Parks in one of the most fascinating settings of the United States.

Superintendent
Everglades National Park

This first guide to a local but unique and fascinating region has become a reality because of the fine cooperation of the Florida National Parks and Monuments Association, Inc. (formerly the Everglades Natural History Assn.), and the staff of the Everglades National Park, especially Warren F. Hamilton, Jack B. Dodd, William B. Robertson, Tom Gilbert and Ernst J. Christensen. Expert assistance came from R. Tucker Abbott, Robert P. Allen, George Stevenson, Alexander Sprunt IV, Don Hoffmeister, Hobart Smith, and Don Poppenhager. Thanks are due to the artist and to the photographers credited below. H.S.Z.

1992 Edition
© Copyright 1960 by Golden Press, Inc. All rights reserved, including the right of reproduction in whole or in part in any form. Designed and produced by Artists and Writers Press, Inc. Printed in the U.S.A. by Western Publishing Company, Inc. Published by Golden Press, New York, New York. ISBN: 0-307-24005-3.

PHOTO CREDITS: William Craighead, p. 16; Everglades National Park, pp. 13, 15, 17, 18 (bottom), 66, 72, 75; Florida State News Bureau, pp. 8, 14, 19, 20, 25, 73; National Audubon Society by George Porter, p. 71; Herbert S. Zim, pp. 12, 18 (top), 69, 70, 84.

Golden®, A Golden Guide®, and Golden Press®
are trademarks of Western Publishing Company, Inc.

CONTENTS

TAMIAMI TRAIL

EDGE OF MANGROVES

41

Big
Nation
LO

Everglades

TEN THOUSAND ISLANDS

Lopez R.

Gu
Slo

PAVILION KEY

Chevelier Bay

Alligator
Bay

TURKEY KEY

ONION

B
Los

Lostmans R.

HIGHLAND POINT

Rodgers R.

Broad R.

Harney R.

Ponce
de Leon
Bay

Oyster
Bay

W
W

N. W. Cape

CAPE
SABLE

Jo

Gator
La

Lake Ingraham

F

East Cape

GULF

OF

MEXICO

BIG
PINE
KEY

Marathon

VA

BAHIA
HONDA
KEY

SADDLEBUNCH
KEYS

Key West

BOCA
CHICA
KEY

F L O R I D

4

SUNSHINE STATE PARKWAY

27   95
821
Miami

TAMIAMI TRAIL   41   Miami Beach

Shark Valley Road

27

Everglades National Park

PINEWOODS TRAIL

EDGE OF PINELANDS

LONG PINE KEY   LONG PINE KEY CAMP

Homestead
Florida City

ROYAL PALM STATION   VISITORS CENTER ANHINGA TRAIL   VISITOR CENTER

GUMBO LIMBO TRAIL

Taylor Slough

Biscayne Bay

BISCAYNE NATIONAL PARK

N

W   E

S

Joe Bay   Barnes Sound

Cuthbert Lake Rookery

Black Water Sound

KEY LARGO

0   5   10   20
Miles

FLORIDA   BAY

John Pennekamp Coral Reef State Park

Tavernier

PLANTATION KEY

LEGEND

1   UPPER MATECUMBE KEY

– – –   Park Boundaries

LOWER MATECUMBE KEY

LONG KEY   K E Y S

Surfaced Road

K   E   Y   S

5

This region, like a good stew, is a subtle blend of several ingredients. To understand this unique and delightful area, which actually extends from Lake Okeechobee south, keep in mind the following factors:

NEARNESS TO THE TROPICS Key West lies just about one degree from the Tropic of Cancer ($23\frac{1}{2}°$ N. Lat.) which marks the beginning of the tropics. The Everglades extend north to about 27°. Miami is south of Cairo, Bagdad, and Delhi—farther south than any other large U.S. city on the North American continent.

CLIMATE reflects the region's nearness to the tropics. This area does not have the four typical seasons of the temperate zone, but has a two-season climate. The warm, wet season lasts from May to November. This is a time of short, heavy showers which produce most of the 50 to 60 inches of annual rainfall in the Everglades. This is also the hurricane season. The cool, dry season lasts from December through April, and while the average temperature is about 70° for January, northern cold fronts occasionally push south. These may bring disastrous frosts. Plant and animal life respond to the cold and dryness. The Everglades are less green and the animals are harder to find. The Everglades climate in general is influenced more by tropical factors than by temperate ones.

CLIMATIC DATA FOR SOME SOUTH FLORIDA PLACES

Place	Avg. Jan. Temp.	Avg. July Temp.	Highest Temp.	Lowest Temp.	Avg. Rainfall
Miami	68°	82°	98°	27°	59 in.
Homestead	67	81	98	26	62
Everglades	67	82	100	28	55
Long Key	70	84	99	37	44
Key West	70	83	100	41	38

Trade winds moderate local climate.

TRADE WINDS blowing from the southeast are a factor in giving the region a near-tropical climate. They (and hurricanes) bring seeds of plants and even some small animals from the West Indies. Many plants and animals in the Everglades and Keys are of West Indies origin.

HURRICANES are "big winds," 75 miles an hour or more, circling a low pressure area. They swing up from the tropics during the wet season, growing on the energy of the warm, moist, oceanic air. One was estimated to expend energy at the rate of 27 billion horsepower. Hurricanes, though dangerous, also have a positive effect on this region. Torrential rains flood the Everglades and replenish the water supply. The ocean sweeping inland opens new channels, and often brings insects and other animals from the Caribbean, enriching the area.

FIRE, usually considered only in terms of its destruction, has a positive side, too, in this area. In the pinelands (p. 16) periodic fires clear the area of some plants and encourage the growth of others, thus helping to establish and maintain certain natural communities.

DRAINAGE in a region less than ten feet above sea level would hardly seem important, but it is. Tremendous amounts of water once moved slowly through the Everglades, funneled down from the Lake Okeechobee area. Both coasts of south Florida are slightly elevated and the great trough of the Everglades acts as a broad, shallow, grass-clogged river to the sea. The natural drainage of the Everglades has been altered by canals, mostly dug from 1905-60. Less water from the northern Everglades now enters the Park. Growing agriculture and urban water usage places increased demands on the finite quantity of water in the Park, making it more difficult to maintain the wetlands ecosystem.

TERRAIN The actual form of the land also determines the character of this region. Limestone is the only rock. In some places, slightly higher ridges make the environment a bit different. Sinkholes form ponds which later become filled with muck and soil. The honeycombed limestone is saturated with water and acts as a great reservoir, not only for the Everglades but also for Miami and nearby towns. This water is carried down the Keys to Key West in a large pipe.

Natural channels and artificial canals cut the Everglades.

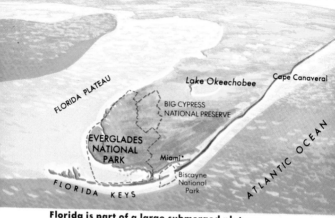

Florida is part of a large submerged plateau.

HOW SOUTH FLORIDA WAS FORMED

Deep below the Everglades and Keys are the ancient rocks which make up the Appalachian Mountains. Ages ago, these were worn level, and the sea has flowed over them many times. At each flooding, new layers of lime and sand have formed. These now lie over the old basement rocks like a geologic layer cake. The top is a layer of limestone formed not long ago during an inter-glacial period. This recent rock, the Miami Oolite, lies under the Everglades. It is a limestone rock composed of tiny round concretions. Rains and underground waters have dissolved and cut into the oolite, pitting the surface. In the northwest part of the Park a slightly older rock, the Tamiami sandy-limestone, comes to the surface to form hammocks. Much of the Keys are the remains of an old coral reef, the Key Largo Limestone. This formed at about the same time as the Miami Oolite, during a long period of retreating ice in the north and rising seas in the south.

Key West

The rocks of southern Florida were formed within the past 50,000 years

FLORIDA KEYS

Gray   Miami Oolite
Pink   Key Largo Limestone
Yellow Recent Lime Ooze and Sand

THE FLORIDA PLATEAU, now two-thirds beneath the sea, developed as layers of rock, half a mile to a mile thick, were formed over the old rock core. Slight changes in the sea level now would mean great changes in the land area. A rise of a few feet could wipe out the Everglades; an equivalent fall could double their size. These movements of the sea are slow, taking thousands of years. There is evidence that the sea is rising, perhaps at a rate rapid enough to cause alarm within the next few decades.

OLD SHORELINES in south Florida show how the sea has advanced and retreated in the past. A fine example now stands 25 feet above sea level. These earth movements, which helped form south Florida during the past million years, still continue. The Miami Oolite was formed as a limy ooze behind the protecting coral reef which is now the Florida Keys. Today a new reef has formed. Behind it, in shallow water and in Florida Bay, the same kind of lime ooze is being deposited.

Besides the rising sea, no other major natural changes in south Florida have marked the past centuries. The man-made changes of the past 50 years have affected the drainage and the shoreline. These, together with land clearing and building, are altering the pattern of native plant and animal life, but not the region itself.

FOSSILS of shellfish, coral, and other small marine animals help tell the story of the formation of this land. In the older rocks, the fossils are less like the animals of today. In the Miami Oolite and Key Largo Limestone, the fossils of coral and shellfish are very similar to animals now living in Florida waters. Fossils tell about the climate as well as the age of rocks. Fossils of tropical plants and animals found in cold regions show that these areas once had a warmer climate. Fossils of mastodons and mammoths in Florida prove that these northern animals moved south as the great ice sheet advanced.

Deposits of peat, formed from fairly recent plants, are now found submerged in several places. This is evidence that the sea is slowly rising and covering what was drier land five or ten thousand years ago.

Fossil Invertebrates from Miami Oolite

THE EVERGLADES is new land, recently formed. It comprises over seven million acres. Much of the northern part is muck soil, which, when drained and fertilized, produces valuable crops. Southward the soil is rockier, but even here, with special treatment, high crop yields can be obtained. Finally, great stretches cannot be used for agriculture because of too little soil and too much water. In this land—the "natural Everglades" is the Everglades National Park.

Approaching the Park, land converted to agricultural use may be seen. In season, note the fields of winter tomatoes and beans. To the north, near Lake Okeechobee the crops are more diversified. Corn, beans, squash, eggplant, celery and melons are harvested for northern markets. Huge areas of sugar cane can be seen from Route 27 south and east of Clewiston.

To convert 'Glades muckland into farmland, over 500 miles of major canals and many more smaller ditches have been dug. Programs of irrigation, insect control, and plant breeding have paid off. Here is intensive, high-production agriculture. To this, the "natural Everglades" of the Park with its native communities of plant and animal life, stand in strong contrast.

Miles of winter vegetables cover Everglades rockland.

Cypress head near Tamiami Trail

NATURAL COMMUNITIES

The Everglades and Keys display, to the discerning eye, a variety of natural communities, each showing distinctions in its plant and animal life. These are produced by differences in the soil and rock structure and small differences in elevation—perhaps only a foot or less. The ocean determines the type of shore or beach and, as it penetrates inland, the saltiness of the water available to plants and animals. Grass and forest fires eliminate certain plants and the newly burnt-over land favors others. All these factors bring variety to the region.

BALD CYPRESS COMMUNITIES lie along the north edge of the park, towards and past Lake Okeechobee. Amid these towering timber trees are nesting grounds for birds such as anhinga and wood stork. Corkscrew Swamp (an Audubon Refuge) is a fine example. Few of the great cypress swamps still remain in Florida. In the Park, pond cypress (p. 52) is more common amid sawgrass and around hammocks.

Egrets feeding in an Everglades slough

THE EVERGLADES is called "a river of grass"—sawgrass (p. 58) dotted by hammocks and tree islands that extend mile after mile. The deeper ponds, sloughs and drainage courses hold water all year, and shelter gar, alligators, otters, and many wading birds. The Anhinga Trail penetrates such a slough. The willows and pond apples along its border are typical.

The water level of the Everglades changes seasonally. During the dry winter and spring, water is low and animal life moves into the sloughs. Fire danger is greater then, and near the sea the salt water penetrates farther inland. With the summer and fall rains, the Everglades floods. Tiny plants and invertebrates teem in the warm shallows. Fish spawn, and there is an abundance of food for birds and larger animals. The fluctuation of the seasons and the direct effects of storms and hurricanes are reflected in the life of the Everglades. Drainage canals dug to protect farmland have affected the sea of grass, also. Along the Tamiami Trail the Everglades can be visited in airboats which skim over the grass and water.

Mahogany Hammock in Everglades National Park

HAMMOCKS are isolated stands of hardwood trees and associated plants in the Everglades and Keys. They form on slightly elevated ground, on old ridges or beaches, or even on Indian mounds. The trees often bear air plants and orchids (pp. 60-61) when the hammocks are moist. Drier hammocks are more open and may include yucca and several kinds of cacti (p. 55). Many more smaller tree islands dot the sawgrass. These have a more limited range of plant and animal life.

It is in the hammocks that the greatest variety of tropical plant and animal life may be found. Moist hammocks support rare ferns as well as orchids and rare tropical plants. During spring migrations, warblers and other songbirds stop here to rest and feed; some remain to nest. Zebra butterflies and other insects abound, and here one finds tree snails *(Liguus)* and other species. Hammocks are found on the Keys, also. Those on North Key Largo are best known. But on the Keys many of the hammocks are being ruthlessly cleared, and the great stands of tropical hardwoods are becoming rare.

PINELANDS mark much of the South, but pine forests on limestone are a rarity. Such pineland communities are found in the Everglades National Park and on Big Pine Key. Slash pine (p. 52) is associated with zamia, palmetto, sumach, smilax, and many smaller plants. Here one may see Virginia deer (Key deer on Big Pine Key), pileated woodpeckers, and other smaller mammals and songbirds. The rich Redlands farming area and much of Miami were once pinelands. Fires, always a danger in our parks, have helped to develop and maintain this type of open pine forest by destroying seedlings of other plants. Without fire, hardwoods take over.

Sunset in Everglades pinelands

Mangroves near Paurotis Palm Pond

MANGROVES flourish on ocean shores and so mark much of the coast in the Park and Keys. They form dense, almost impenetrable thickets with high prop roots and interlaced branches. These offer shelter to pelicans, cormorants, herons, ibis, and other wading birds. Most of the great bird rookeries are located in mangroves. With the mangroves (p. 50) grow buttonwood and a few other salt-resistant plants. Many of the smaller islands in the Keys are mangrove islands. The land itself, perhaps only a few inches above sea level, looks like a tropical paradise because of the mangrove cover. Closer, it is much less attractive, except to birds.

Mangroves do not cover all the shores. Some are rocky or sandy beaches (p. 18). These shores may merge into a coastal prairie of salt-tolerant grasses and flowering plants. Sometimes isolated black mangroves and buttonwoods are present. Yucca, agave and native cacti may form thickets. The prairie is more likely to be on marl soil, and here killdeer, plovers, stilts, terns, and other shore birds may nest.

Rocky beach on Plantation Key

ROCKY SHORES, cut and eroded into jagged patterns, are formed by wave and chemical action on exposed coral limestone. Sea urchins, chitons and other shellfish live in crevices, and smaller shore birds are constantly feeding. Use care; you can easily turn an ankle while exploring these rough beaches.

SANDY BEACHES occur at Cape Sable, where most of the sand is crushed shell, and along the Keys from Islamorada south. They harbor more and different plants and less animal life than the rocky beaches. Coconuts, seagrape, buttonwood and seven-year apple may be present, and many smaller, salt-tolerant plants.

Shell beach at Cape Sable

CORAL REEFS found within Biscayne National Park and bordering the Keys provide a nearby underwater community of plant and animal life which is literally "out of this world." Glass-bottom boats, snorkeling and diving equipment open the way to this undersea land. Those who make the effort to see it never forget the experience or regret the effort. Many square miles of reefs are protected within National and State Preserves. The reefs abound with invertebrates, in addition to living coral, and are the home of many kinds of tropical fishes—parrotfish, angelfish, morays, triggerfish and the like.

Within Everglades and Biscayne National Parks and the Keys are extensive areas of submerged land. Mile after mile lies under only a few feet of water. In this submerged land live many kinds of crustaceans and shellfish. Smaller fishes spawn here, too, making this a feeding ground for shore and water birds. Herons and egrets snap up small fishes. Terns, ospreys, pelicans and gulls dive after fishes, also. Spoonbills may feed in tidal sloughs.

Coral reef fishes, Florida Keys

THE KEYS stretch in a long, 200-mile arc from Miami south and west to the Dry Tortugas. Scores of islands, the largest (Key Largo) about 35 miles long, dot Florida Bay or extend as a long chain separating the Gulf of Mexico from the Atlantic. The Keys are not a natural plant and animal community like those on the previous pages. All the community types, except the Everglades itself, are found here, with mangroves, hammocks and beaches predominating. On the Keys the oceanic, tropical climate is accentuated, making this a vacation area without equal in the United States. Here the fishing is famous—in the bays and inlets, on the shallow bottoms, along the reefs and in the deep blue of the Gulf Stream. The varied plant and animal life, plus the unusual scenery, emphasize the Keys as an extension of the Park—and down to Long Key, the Park boundary does follow the Inland Waterway. Visit Biscayne National Park, John Pennekamp Coral Reef State Park on Key Largo, Key Deer National Wildlife Refuge on Big Pine Key, historic spots in Key West, and, if possible, Ft. Jefferson on the Dry Tortugas.

The Florida Keys are a chain of islands.

KEY DEER, a dwarf race of the white-tailed deer, is usually 25 to 30 in. high and weighs about 50 lbs. These rare deer (once almost extinct) are found on or near Big Pine Key. A refuge has been established for their protection.

ANIMAL LIFE

Animal life (and plant life, too) balance the seascapes and vistas to make the Everglades and Keys so attractive. Everglades National Park was created primarily to preserve a biologic environment. Here are rookeries of wading birds along with scores of others—some, West Indian in origin. Here also are mammals, from lithe panthers to finger-sized shrews. Alligators and crocodiles are found, and many other unusual reptiles, frogs, and toads. The waters abound with fish, so sports-fishing and skin-diving (in deeper water) are famous. In the sea, on land, and even in the trees are shells (mollusks). Look for them and, while looking, don't miss the great array of small animal life—butterflies and other insects and small marine animals of fresh and salt water. The beauty in color and form of the smallest plants and animals makes it well worth the time to seek them out.

FLORIDA PANTHER or COUGAR is the largest of the wild cats. Panthers are 6-7 ft. long and are tawny colored with black ears. An endangered species of great concern, panthers feed on deer and small animals.

BOBCAT, less than half the size of the cougar, is much more common. In the 'Glades it is darker and larger than to the north. Hunts at night but may be seen at dusk near Flamingo by visitors.

RACCOON, with its black mask and ringed tail, is a night prowler of mangroves and pinelands. Seen along roads and near camps. Locally the raccoon is pale, quite yellow, and not strongly marked.

WHITE-TAILED DEER is the common Virginia deer of the East. It is hunted north of the Park and is an important game animal. Only males have antlers. Feeds on leaves, twigs, and wild fruits.

MANGROVE SQUIRREL, the local form of the fox squirrel, is larger than the gray squirrel, also found here. Note the white feet, dark back, variable color. Nests in hollow trees.

MARSH RABBIT is a small all-brown rabbit seen along the Tamiami Trail and in the Everglades. It is smaller than the cottontail and lacks the white markings. Feeds on marsh grasses.

ROUND-TAILED MUSKRAT is not the southern fur-bearer but is a smaller mammal nesting in mangrove roots and in marsh grasses. This fine swimmer is also called the Florida water rat.

OPOSSUM is a pouched mammal, distantly related to the kangaroo, and the only one of its kind in this country. Common in drier woodlands and hammocks. Has 8-12 very small young in one litter.

OTTER is a water-loving carnivore related to weasels and skunks. Lives along sloughs, feeding on fish and other small animals. The otter is an intelligent, playful beast with fine, heavy fur. Males grow up to 5 ft. long and weigh up to 30 lbs. Females smaller.

COTTON RAT is a southern rodent, common, but not often seen in the Park. Lives in meadows, along ditches and in farmland, feeding on all kinds of plant material. They damage sugar cane and other crops. May have 6 litters a year.

MANATEE or sea cow is a large (10-12 ft.), timid, ungainly aquatic mammal found in Florida bays and inlets where it feeds on water plants. Forelegs are flippers. Manatees cannot stand prolonged cold. An endangered species.

BOTTLENOSED DOLPHINS live in Florida waters. Most often seen as the stars at aquarium shows. Here they leap high for food and have learned to perform remarkable tricks. Length to 10 ft.; wt. 200 lbs. or more.

Common Egret feeding in water lilies

BIRDS are the star attractions of the Everglades and Keys, a region famous for its rookeries. Besides the conspicuous wading birds, land birds, water birds and birds of prey also abound. Some kinds found here are not seen elsewhere in this country. Identify those illustrated on the next pages. Also look for the rarer mangrove cuckoo and smooth-billed ani. The Everglades National Park records some 300 species; a check list is available at the Visitors' Center. All birds are protected in the Park, and nearly all outside. Disturbing birds by approaching rookeries in boats may do more harm than hunting. To see birds better, try Park tours. Watch patiently at roadside stations in the Park and at vantage points along the Keys. Binoculars are a help.

PAINTED BUNTING is a brilliant, gay, sparrow-like bird seen in winter. Male pictured below. Female yellow and greenish.

COOTS are black, duck-like, with small heads, white bills and lobed feet. They are closely related to the gallinule (p. 26). Commonly seen swimming and feeding in shallow waters in winter.

BIRDS 25

White Pelican

Brown Pelican

Cormorant

Anhinga

Purple Gallinule

BROWN PELICAN is common. It is large, silvery-brown, with a long, flat, pouched bill. It dives for fish in coastal waters.

WHITE PELICAN is a larger winter visitor with black on its wings; often seen inland. Scoops up fish in shallow water.

CORMORANT is a large, duck-like bird, shiny black with an orange throat pouch. Often seen perched upright over the water.

PURPLE GALLINULE, a delight to watch, is a yellow-legged, purple and green marsh bird with a striking yellow-tipped red bill.

ANHINGA or water turkey, is a large, slender bird with a long tail and a longer neck, seen along canals and sloughs. It is an excellent swimmer. Male is illustrated; female is browner.

Little Blue Heron

Green-Backed Heron

LITTLE BLUE HERON is almost black with dark bill and legs. Seen mainly around fresh water. Young are white.

GREEN-BACKED HERON is smaller, green and blue, with reddish neck. Raises its crest when frightened. Legs are yellow or orange.

NIGHT HERONS The black-crowned, most common, has a black back, white below. Yellow-crowned is rarer; blue-gray body.

LIMPKIN is an odd, spotted marsh bird with a slightly turned-down bill. Feeds mainly on snails. Now becoming more common.

AMERICAN BITTERN is a shy, nondescript marsh bird, stocky, mottled brown with black wing tips. When frightened it "freezes" with bill erect. Found mainly in marsh grasses in winter.

Black-Crowned Night Heron

Limpkin

American Bittern

Snowy Egret

SNOWY EGRET, one of the smaller egrets (to 28 in.), with yellow feet, is a very active feeder. Bill and legs are black. The Cattle Egret with yellow bill and legs and buff back is becoming increasingly common. It is about the same size as the Snowy Egret.

Common Egret

COMMON EGRET is the medium-sized egret (to 43 in.) of this area. Note the black legs and yellow beak. Once on the verge of extinction, these birds and the Snowy Egrets have come back and are now common.

GREAT WHITE HERON (to 54 in.) is now believed to be a white phase of the Great Blue Heron (p. 30). Note the yellow beak and yellowish legs. It lives mainly in Florida Bay.

REDDISH EGRET (30 in.) is most common on the Keys. It appears as a white phase or gray with rusty head and neck. Both have a black-tipped, pink bill. Feathers often fluffed and fuzzy.

Great White Heron

Reddish Egret

28

WHITE IBIS is a handsome all-white bird (25 in.) with a red face and turned-down bill which marks all other ibises as well. Wing tips are black. Often seen in flight at Duck Rock. Nests in large rookeries with the white herons or near their nests.

WOOD STORK, large and majestic (to 47 in.), was formerly called Wood Ibis. Note its heavier bill, half-black wings and naked head. Flies with neck outstretched like ibises. Locally called Flintheads.

FLAMINGOS are seldom seen except in captivity. Occur in West Indies and Bahamas, but rare in Florida. Large (45 in.) with long neck, long legs, and a heavy "Roman" beak.

ROSEATE SPOONBILL, seen in the Everglades and Keys, is the only large (32 in.) pink bird with a flattened bill. Eats by swinging bill from side to side. Young birds are paler.

White Ibis

Wood Stork

Flamingos

Roseate
Spoonbill

GREAT BLUE HERON (54 in.) is like the Great White Heron (p. 28) except for its dark color. It occurs much more widely.

TRICOLORED HERON (26 in.), formerly called the Louisiana Heron, is blue-gray with a white belly which distinguishes it from the little blue heron.

LAUGHING GULL, named for its raucous call, has a black head (in summer) and black wing tips. Very common. Size, 16 in.

ROYAL TERN is a gull-like bird with a deeply-forked tail and orange bill. Several other terns are roughly similar. Length, 20 in.

FRIGATE BIRD or man-o'-war bird (40 in.) sails with scarcely a wing movement, then dives to snatch food from gulls. Male is black; female is white below; tails are deeply-forked.

SWALLOW-TAILED KITE (24 in.) is seen on the wing over the 'Glades in summer. Black and white, with deeply-forked tail.

OSPREY or fishhawk (24 in.) hovers in the wind and dives for fish. Compare with bald eagle (below). Osprey has a white belly.

STILT (15 in.) is one of many thin-legged shore birds. White below, black above, bill slightly upturned. Found in marshes.

RED-SHOULDERED HAWK, seen along all marshlands, has white bands on its dark tail. Length to 23 in., reddish shoulders.

BALD EAGLE, once common along shores, has a white head and tail when mature. Young lack white. Larger than the osprey (32-36 in.) and with a dark underside. Feeds mainly on fishes.

BLACK-WHISKERED VIREO is similar to red-eyed except for line of black on its throat. Breeds in mangroves and hammocks.

GRAY KINGBIRD of the shores and Keys has a larger bill than other eastern kingbirds, and a notched tail. W. I. species. 9 in.

BOAT-TAILED GRACKLE (16 in.) is common along the water. Note its long tail and glossy plumage. Female is smaller and brown.

PILEATED WOODPECKER (17 in.), large, black and crested, is seen mainly in cypress and pine, and in hardwood hammocks.

WHITE-CROWNED PIGEON (14 in.), a large dark bird with a white crown, is found mainly on the Keys in summer. Feeds on wild fruits. Lays 2 white eggs in crude nests in mangrove and other trees.

SNAKES and other reptiles, including several unique kinds of lizards, are found in the Everglades and the Keys. Most snake stories are exaggerated. These unusual animals are no more common or dangerous here than in other southern areas. Snakes are protected in the Park. Most kinds are harmless. Leave all of them alone. Dangerous species are illustrated on p. 35. Snakes feed on rodents, insects, frogs, lizards, and small fish.

GREEN SNAKE of this area is the rough species, marked by a ridge on each of its scales. Avg. length about 30 in. This is a docile, insect-eating snake of grasslands and open woods.

EVERGLADES RACER, or black snake, is common in drier areas of the 'Glades and Keys. It feeds mainly on lizards, other snakes, insects, rodents and birds. Note the white chin. Average length, 4 ft.

INDIGO SNAKE, the largest snake found in the Park, grows to 8 ft. However, it is harmless, feeding mainly on rodents. A heavier snake than the black racer. Often used by snake charmers.

EVERGLADES RAT SNAKE found in the Park, is very similar to the yellow rat snake, common all through the South. But it is more orange in color, with dark stripes vague or lacking. Found in 'Glades or salt marshes, sometimes in trees. Feeds mainly on rodents.

COACHWHIP is a long (to 7 ft.) slender snake of southern fields and prairies. Color is variable, but darker at the head and lighter towards the tail. Feeds on rodents, lizards and birds. Female lays about a dozen eggs in summer Young are spotted.

BANDED WATER SNAKE is common in south Florida. On young snakes the dark blotches on the back often have light oval spots. Older snakes are duller and the markings darker. Compare with water moccasin (p. 35) which has facial pits on its wider head.

MANGROVE WATER SNAKE, like above, has a flattened tail and a row of light belly spots. May be found near salt water. Water snakes feed on frogs, toads and small fishes. In turn, they are food of wading birds, turtles, larger snakes, and mammals.

EVERGLADES SWAMP SNAKE is one example of the many smaller snakes of the region. It is 16 to 20 in., striped, with a yellowish belly marked by a central row of black spots. This is a snake of lakes and waterways, often seen in beds of water hyacinths.

PIGMY RATTLER, also called ground rattler, is a small species rarely over 2 ft. long. It is gray-brown, marked with darker blotches. Despite its small size it bites, and its bite is serious. These rattlers prefer drier ground, but are often near water.

WATER MOCCASIN (Cottonmouth) should not be confused with harmless water snakes (p. 34). It is thick bodied and has no rattle. The head is pitted, wide at the base. These water-loving snakes feed on frogs, snakes, fish and small mammals.

CORAL SNAKE small (avg. 2 ft.) and attractive, is timid, and does not bite readily. Its bite, however, is very poisonous. Note its black nose and rings of yellow, black and red which completely encircle the body. Several harmless snakes look similar.

EASTERN DIAMONDBACK is our largest rattler and hence quite dangerous. Average length, 5 ft. Note diamond pattern on back, triangular head, with no plates on top, and the tell-tale rattle. Found in hammocks and open country. Feeds mainly on rodents.

SNAKE BITE is more easily prevented than treated. Wear heavy shoes and use care when walking. All snakes bite. The bite of non-poisonous species may show a U-shaped pattern of tooth marks. Treat with an antiseptic. Bites of poisonous snakes often show two large fang punctures, and perhaps other teeth marks as well. Learn first aid *before* you go. Carry a snake bite kit. Keep the patient quiet; apply a tourniquet; cut and suck the wound. Notify a Park ranger or get the victim to a doctor immediately.

Skink

Whip-Tail Lizard

TURTLES—over a dozen kinds—live in this region. Illustrated below are two land species, two fresh-water species, and, finally, two marine species. Fresh-water species are the most common. Most turtles are harmless; a few snap viciously. Depending on the species, fresh-water turtles feed on insects, fish, fruits and berries, while sea turtles feed on marine plants and invertebrates. All sea turtles are endangered/protected species, due to loss of nesting and feeding habitat and exploitation for food and shells.

Green Turtle
(marine)

Soft-Shelled Turtle
(fresh-water)

Red-Bellied Slider
(fresh-water)

Anole

Glass Snake

Ashy Gecko

LIZARDS in this area are common, swift, and attractive. None are poisonous. Practically all feed on insects and other small animals. A few rare species of West Indian origin are found on the Keys. Here, five of the more common species are illustrated. The anole, or American chameleon, is sometimes sold at circuses. It does change its color slowly, but may not eat well in captivity and hence does not make a good pet.

Box Turtle (land)

Loggerhead Turtle (marine)

Gopher Turtle (land)

Alligator

ALLIGATORS AND CROCODILES are found wild in the Everglades National Park, the only place in the U.S. where they occur together. Alligators prefer the fresh-water sloughs, feeding on fishes, turtles, birds and other small animals. Note their darker color, broader head, and teeth which are mostly covered when the mouth is closed. Large alligators are now rare, and all are protected.

Crocodiles are much rarer than alligators in this region. They live in the salt marshes and mangroves of the Park and Keys, sometimes going out into Florida Bay. They are thinner, with a narrower, pointed snout. Some teeth are exposed when their mouth is closed. Crocodiles are more dangerous than alligators, but are too rare in this country to be the problem they are in Asia and Africa. Both crocodiles and alligators lay several dozen eggs which are hatched mainly by the heat of the sun.

Crocodile

GREEN TREE FROG is a bright-green member of the tree frog family. It has a light stripe along the side, and relatively long legs. Undersides are white. Some may have yellow spots on the back. Found in swamps and near ponds, perched on debris or leaves of aquatic plants.

CUBAN TREE FROG is the largest tree frog in the United States, 3 to 5 in. long, with large discs at the ends of fingers and toes. This unusual frog is common on the Keys gathering near lights at night to catch insects. It is widespread in the Park.

NARROW-MOUTHED TOAD is an unusual, small, smooth-skinned frog with a narrow, pointed head and a fold of skin across the back of its neck. It often has a light line down the sides. Female lighter and larger than male.

PIG FROG (Southern Bullfrog) is the main Florida source of frog legs. It is large (to 6 in.), olive green and tan, yellowish below. Hunted at night by froggers in air-boats in lakes, ponds, and wet prairies out-side the Park.

SIREN, an odd salamander of ponds, ditches and canals, has small front legs only and conspicuous external gills. Body dark gray, greenish or black, sometimes mot-tled, with yellow spots on sides. Length, 2-3 ft.

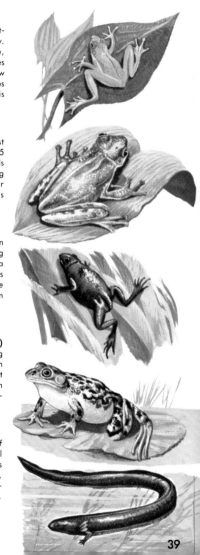

39

LARGEMOUTH BASS (a sunfish) is the region's gamest fresh-water fish. Weighing to 15 lbs. and more, it is hooked in lakes, canals and slow streams. Its large mouth extends beyond the eyes.

FISHES, to thousands of sportsmen, are the only animals worthy of attention in the Everglades and Keys. And, in all fairness, this *is* an internationally famous fishing area. Most of over 1,000 species of Florida fishes are found in Florida Bay and the nearby Gulf and ocean. The fishes of the coral reefs are magnificent, and the undersea life in the Keys is so exciting and breath-taking that it is truly another world.

MOSQUITOFISH, or Gambusia, named for its food, is an example of a dozen small fish species which are important links in the Everglades web of life. This 2-in. fish lives in fresh and brackish waters.

FLORIDA GAR is an ancient fish, common in sloughs. It is long, cylindrical, with a long, narrow jaw and large, heavy scales. Gars have a lung-like swim bladder aiding their gills.

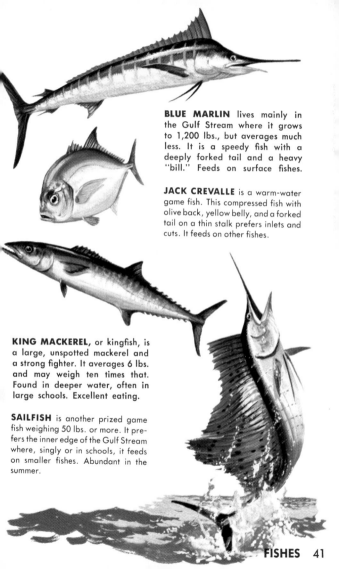

BLUE MARLIN lives mainly in the Gulf Stream where it grows to 1,200 lbs., but averages much less. It is a speedy fish with a deeply forked tail and a heavy "bill." Feeds on surface fishes.

JACK CREVALLE is a warm-water game fish. This compressed fish with olive back, yellow belly, and a forked tail on a thin stalk prefers inlets and cuts. It feeds on other fishes.

KING MACKEREL, or kingfish, is a large, unspotted mackerel and a strong fighter. It averages 6 lbs. and may weigh ten times that. Found in deeper water, often in large schools. Excellent eating.

SAILFISH is another prized game fish weighing 50 lbs. or more. It prefers the inner edge of the Gulf Stream where, singly or in schools, it feeds on smaller fishes. Abundant in the summer.

FISHES 41

SNOOK, a prized sport fish, is caught in Florida Bay canals and "rivers." Hard to catch but excellent eating.

MANGROVE SNAPPER, similar to the red snapper, is a prized game fish and a wary fighter of Key channels, mangroves and flats. Wt., 5 lbs. or more.

BONEFISH move in and out of Keys shallows where they are top game fish. Wt., to 5 lbs. or more. Bony, so rarely eaten.

MULLET, fine eating; is caught commercially outside the park. A plant eater, it does not take bait but is a fine bait for large game fish.

TARPON, averaging about 30 lbs., are hooked in the Keys and Bay in spring. This fine sports fish is rarely used as food. The scales, unusually large, clearly show growth rings.

UTTERFLYFISH feeds on small nimals in the reefs. Length, to 8 in. lote black bar through eye and spot ear tail.

TRIGGERFISH is so called because of the odd locking action of its dorsal spine for defense. A tough, leathery fish of coral bottoms. Wt., to 5 lbs.

FRENCH ANGELFISH is common in the Keys. Note flecks of yellow on sides and at base of tail. Gray angelfish lacks this yellow. Several other small- and medium-sized angelfish are found.

ERGEANT-MAJOR and other shes on this page live in coral reefs. his one (6 in.) is common in small chools along the Keys.

ARROTFISH The rainbow parrot nd several others live in Key reefs. ttractive fishes which create sand by ushing corals. Wt., to 20 lbs.

ZEBRA, a unique butterfly, lives in hammocks and woods. The shape is typical of many tropical butterflies.

ANIMALS WITHOUT BACKBONES

The world over, the smaller, simpler animals without backbones are the most common—and perhaps the most important. This is especially true in the Everglades, for warm climate favors such animals. Some, like the mosquitoes, will plague visitors. Most have no direct effect on man one way or another. They feed on smaller life and are, in turn, the food of larger. The interested visitor to the Park and the Keys can find many rare kinds of butterflies and other insects. Here also are scorpions, millipedes, tree snails, and land crabs. In Florida Bay and the Keys, marine invertebrate life is especially rich. Best known are the mollusks or shelled animals, the starfishes, sea urchins and corals. Many can be collected on the Keys. Look for sea fans, sea worms, and jellyfishes. A few kinds are dangerous because they can sting; more are beautiful and exciting; all are interesting.

LUBBER GRASSHOPPER, largest native species; found in open areas, often in great numbers.

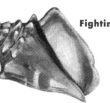
Fighting Conch

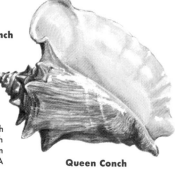
Queen Conch

FIGHTING CONCH is much smaller than the Queen Conch (3-4 in.), usually orange-brown with spines on the last whorl. A south Florida species.

QUEEN CONCH is not only beautiful but the animal is excellent eating. Try conch chowder, a typical dish of the Florida Keys. Length, 6-12 in.

TURKEY WING is a bivalve—a clam-like animal 2-3 in. long with irregular bands of brown. Shells are found on most beaches.

Turkey Wing

ANGEL WING is a large, fragile shell of a bivalve which lives deep in the mud. Good shell specimens are rare, though the animals themselves are common in warmer waters. Length, 4-8 in.

WEST INDIES CHITON is one of several found on rocky shores. These animals have 8 valves in tough, leathery skin. 2-3 in.

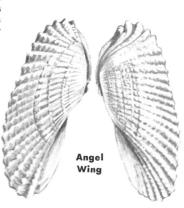
Angel Wing

West Indies Chiton

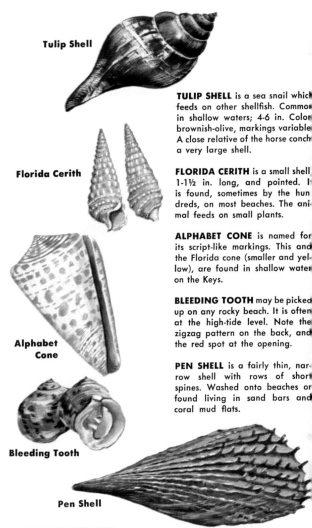

Tulip Shell

TULIP SHELL is a sea snail which feeds on other shellfish. Common in shallow waters; 4-6 in. Color brownish-olive, markings variable. A close relative of the horse conch, a very large shell.

Florida Cerith

FLORIDA CERITH is a small shell, 1-1½ in. long, and pointed. It is found, sometimes by the hundreds, on most beaches. The animal feeds on small plants.

ALPHABET CONE is named for its script-like markings. This and the Florida cone (smaller and yellow), are found in shallow water on the Keys.

BLEEDING TOOTH may be picked up on any rocky beach. It is often at the high-tide level. Note the zigzag pattern on the back, and the red spot at the opening.

Alphabet Cone

PEN SHELL is a fairly thin, narrow shell with rows of short spines. Washed onto beaches or found living in sand bars and coral mud flats.

Bleeding Tooth

Pen Shell

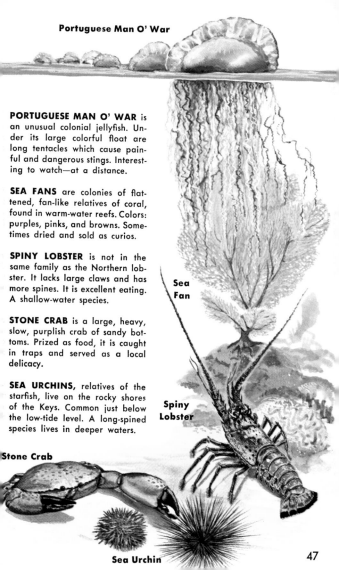

Portuguese Man O' War

PORTUGUESE MAN O' WAR is an unusual colonial jellyfish. Under its large colorful float are long tentacles which cause painful and dangerous stings. Interesting to watch—at a distance.

SEA FANS are colonies of flattened, fan-like relatives of coral, found in warm-water reefs. Colors: purples, pinks, and browns. Sometimes dried and sold as curios.

SPINY LOBSTER is not in the same family as the Northern lobster. It lacks large claws and has more spines. It is excellent eating. A shallow-water species.

STONE CRAB is a large, heavy, slow, purplish crab of sandy bottoms. Prized as food, it is caught in traps and served as a local delicacy.

SEA URCHINS, relatives of the starfish, live on the rocky shores of the Keys. Common just below the low-tide level. A long-spined species lives in deeper waters.

Sea Fan

Spiny Lobster

Stone Crab

Sea Urchin

47

BLUE CRAB is the edible swimming crab of the Atlantic coast. Found on sandy bottoms in inlets and channels.

HERMIT CRAB has no shell of its own, but uses mollusk shells for a home. Some, in the Keys, live on land and even in trees.

TREE SNAILS are found in the Everglades and Keys, but it takes a trained eye to see them. Many varieties, all delicately colored.

APPLE SNAIL, common in marshes and sloughs of south Florida, is the sole food of the Snail Kite, a rare bird of the region.

CORALS are animals related to jellyfish. They build up lime deposits to form reefs and islands. Large reefs extend along the Keys (also an old reef). Staghorn coral is illustrated above.

PLANT LIFE

SPIDER LILIES with narrow, leaves and thin, white-petaled flowers dot wet ground.

Plant life is the great middleman in southern Florida. It uses the land, the water and the climate to make an environment suitable for a rich variety of wildlife — and for visitors, too. In this role, plants react to subtle differences which might easily escape notice. Very slight increases in elevation, less than a foot, will make the land suitable to plants which will not grow a hundred yards away. Slight differences in the amount of salt in the water and soil affects plant life also. These physical variations have created a series of environments (pp. 13-20) in which certain types of plants and animals tend to co-exist.

As for the plants themselves, the number of species is very high. In this area there are about 125 species of woody plants and many more kinds of herbs. There are undoubtedly more kinds of plants than vertebrate animals whose U.S. range is limited to this near-tropic region. These plants range from gumbo-limbo, mahogany and tamarind down through shrubs and flowering plants to ferns and mosses.

Of all the plants, visitors should note the familiar poison ivy (common in hammocks) and the less common but equally potent poisonwood (p. 55). Finally, there is the very rare manchineel, reputedly one of the most poisonous trees in the world. Picking of any plants is prohibited in the Park. Outside, native orchids and roadside plants are protected by state law.

TREES AND SHRUBS of this area are diverse. They include red maple, sweet gum and a few other species which extend down from northern states. They include species widely distributed in the South, such as cypress and magnolias. They also include West Indian species and others not found north of Lake Okeechobee. Most cypress and mahogany have been cut down. There are no large commercial forests left. Some of the remaining rare trees on the Keys are threatened by land clearing. A few species are already extinct.

MANGROVE is a name applied to three different trees.

RED MANGROVE, a tree of bay shores, has spreading branches and high arched prop roots. The simple leathery leaves are dotted with black below. Flowers mature into long woody seedlings before they fall. This is the commonest mangrove.

BLACK MANGROVE is a more massive tree. Simple leaves are downy below, 2-4 in. long. Bark is dark brown and scaly. Flowers are white, very fragrant, and a source of honey. The aerial roots are simple and grow vertically.

WHITE MANGROVE is a buttonwood (p. 53), with leaves opposite and rounded. Thin flower spikes. A tall tree with brown flaky bark. Has no aerial roots.

GUMBO-LIMBO, a quick-growing tropical tree, is easy to spot with its massive trunk and smooth, papery, reddish-brown bark. Leaves have 3-7 leaflets, uneven at the base and pointed at the apex. Small red fruits in summer.

JAMAICA DOGWOOD, or fish-poison tree, was so used. Note compound leaves, pale lavender flowers and winged fruits.

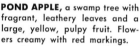

POND APPLE, a swamp tree with fragrant, leathery leaves and a large, yellow, pulpy fruit. Flowers creamy with red markings.

REDBAY has a rough, purplish-brown bark. Leaves are simple, leathery and alternate. Fruit is oval, black, ½ in. long.

COCO-PLUM, a tropical plum, has rounded leaves indented at the tip. Fruit is a pale purple; matures in early fall.

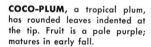

STRANGLER FIG often grows on other trees, strangling them while it takes root. Note thick, oval, alternate leaves and red fruits.

SLASH PINE, a subspecies specific to south Florida; fast-growing, long needles, 2 or 3 to a cluster. Cones with spines on scales.

POND CYPRESS is smaller than bald, with minute, scaly leaves and thin gray bark. Usually lacks "knees" at base of the trunk.

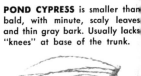

LIVE OAK grows in hammocks but is very rare on the Keys. Acorns small, black. Leaves oval, dark green, and downy beneath.

WEST INDIES MAHOGANY is common in the Park and Keys. Leaves compound, fruits large, and woody, split open from base.

SEA-GRAPE is a stout coastal tree forming huge thickets. Grape-like fruits give it its name. Leaves rounded, thick, red-veined.

BUTTONWOOD is common on all drier shores. Note cone-like fruits, simple rough leaves, and flaky, brown bark.

GEIGER TREE is small with wide, downy leaves and attractive, orange flowers. Most abundant on the Keys and near shores.

WILD TAMARIND of Keys and mainland hammocks has twice-compounded leaves, greenish, candytuft flowers, and broad fruit pods.

TETRAZYGIA is a small tree with narrow, opposite leaves, small white flowers and round, dark fruits. Found in pine lands.

ROYAL POINCIANA, from Madagascar, is a broad-topped tree with smooth gray bark, twice-compounded leaves; great clusters of red flowers in late spring.

SAPODILLA, from Central America, yields chicle for chewing gum, and a brown edible fruit. Oval, evergreen leaves grow in rosettes.

KEY LIME, a small, spiny naturalized citrus, is common on the Keys. Fruits, small and yellow, are the basis of famed Key Lime pie.

AUSTRALIAN PINE is no pine at all. Its needles are young twigs; fruit a small cone. Bark is dark, furrowed, scaly. An exotic species.

WOMAN'S TONGUE, named for its broad, rattling seed pods, has twice-compounded leaves, and tufted flower heads. A weed-tree.

YUCCA, or Spanish bayonet, grows along dry shores and in the Keys. Leaves are long and needle-pointed. Creamy, lily-like flowers form dense spike.

AGAVE is a large stemless yucca-like plant. Some have bluish or striped leaves bordered with spines. Flowers on tall stalks.

DILDO, a native cactus, has loping, three-angled, thorny stems. Cephalocerus, rarer, has rounded, branched stems.

POISONWOOD Native, but dangerous tree; shiny compound leaves (usually 5 leaflets); orange fruits, flaky red-brown bark; highly toxic sap. Avoid it.

LIGNUM VITAE, a small, handsome, blue-flowered tree of the Keys with very heavy wood, is now rare. Compound opposite leaves.

PLANTS 55

PALMS may grow 100 feet tall, but are more closely related to grasses and lilies than they are to pines, oaks, or other trees. Palms are tropical. There are more native species in the Everglades and Keys than in any other part of the United States. About ten species grow here, including a few that are nearly extinct. The coconut palm is not actually native, but it is completely naturalized, and is abundant along beaches.

Dozens of other exotic palms are planted as ornamental and shade trees. One of the best collections of growing palms is in the Fairchild Tropical Garden on the south edge of Miami, easily visited on the way to Everglades National Park. Several of the local native palms are small, with low or prostrate stems. Those illustrated are the larger and the more striking southeast species of the Park and the Keys.

PAUROTIS, 12 to 30 ft. high, grows in clumps. Seen in Park and along Tamiami Trail. Leaves fan-shaped with many curved spines on leaf stems. Trunk is slender, brown, and rough because of persistent leaf stalks.

CABBAGE PALMETTO is the most common native palm, found in the Everglades but more abundant to the north. Fan-shaped leaves, bearing many fine threads; midrib prominent. Round black fruits in clusters.

fruit

COCONUT is widespread through all the tropics and in some areas is the most important plant, providing food, shelter and drink. Fruits are distributed by sea and sprout on beach sands. Trees bear in five to seven years. Coconut plantations once flourished at Key Biscayne, Cape Sable and on the Keys. New varieties of coconut fruit earlier and bear more heavily. Unfortunately a coconut disease discovered at Key West is spreading and is causing concern for south Florida trees.

ROYAL PALM is the largest and most beautiful native species. Now widely planted. Note the smooth, gray, bulging trunk, tapering into a green sheath below the large, feathery leaves.

THATCH PALMS (two species) found on the Keys have narrow trunks with fan-shaped leaves. Leaf stocks lack spines. Flowers in long, drooping clusters become small, round, whitish fruits.

6 mos.

12 mos.

2 yrs.

coconut
cross
section

fruit

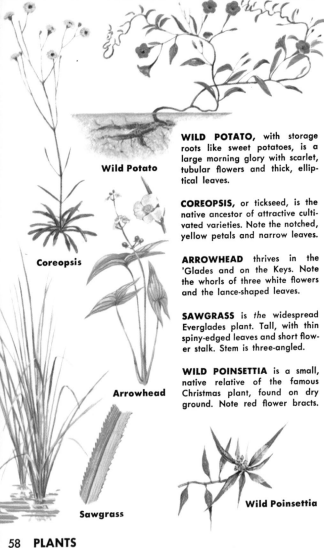

Wild Potato

WILD POTATO, with storage roots like sweet potatoes, is a large morning glory with scarlet, tubular flowers and thick, elliptical leaves.

COREOPSIS, or tickseed, is the native ancestor of attractive cultivated varieties. Note the notched, yellow petals and narrow leaves.

Coreopsis

ARROWHEAD thrives in the 'Glades and on the Keys. Note the whorls of three white flowers and the lance-shaped leaves.

SAWGRASS is *the* widespread Everglades plant. Tall, with thin spiny-edged leaves and short flower stalk. Stem is three-angled.

WILD POINSETTIA is a small, native relative of the famous Christmas plant, found on dry ground. Note red flower bracts.

Arrowhead

Wild Poinsettia

Sawgrass

ZAMIA, or coontie, is a cycad, found in dry, pineland soil. Flowers are cone-like; leaves fern-like. Indians made flour from the underground stems.

Zamia

MOON VINE, a morning glory, is common on burnt-over or bulldozed land. Leaves heart-shaped; flowers flattened.

Moon Vine

RUBBER VINE or wild allamanda is found on the Keys and on dry 'Glade hammocks. A vine with thick, oval, opposite leaves.

RUELLIA is another dry-land plant with blue, tubular, 5-lobed flowers in the axil of the leaf. Leaves are opposite, hairy.

Rubber Vine

BALLOON VINE is named for its thin, swollen, seed capsules. Leaves alternating; three leaflets. Flowers small and whitish.

Ruellia

Balloon Vine

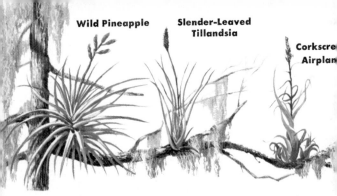

Wild Pineapple

Slender-Leaved Tillandsia

Corkscrew Airplan

AIR PLANTS, or epiphytes, are plants growing free from contact with the ground. They are not parasites. Members of the orchid and pineapple families offer many examples. In south Florida the term is used for wild pineapple and its relatives. Seen on trees along the Tamiami Trail and in the Park. Over a dozen species.

SPANISH MOSS is a member of the pineapple family. Found on oaks and other trees, it bears minute, yellowish flowers which become small, tufted seeds.

BALL or BUNCH MOSS is another epiphyte similar to Spanish moss, but forming irregular balls on twigs and even on telephone wires. Quite common on the Keys.

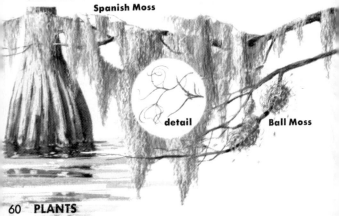

Spanish Moss

detail

Ball Moss

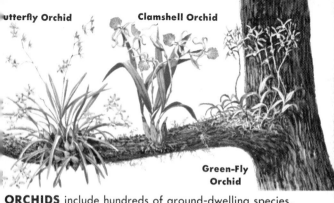

Butterfly Orchid   Clamshell Orchid

Green-Fly Orchid

ORCHIDS include hundreds of ground-dwelling species, but here epiphytic orchids are common on rough-barked trees. These number about a dozen species, including the vanilla orchid which produces vanilla. Most common are several encyclias, illustrated above. The butterfly orchid is delightful; so are the others.

CIGAR ORCHID is a large epiphytic orchid with leaves 1 ft. long and flower stalk up to 5 ft. long. Flowers greenish-yellow, spotted with brown. Rare.

MULE EAR ORCHID is a large, coarse Oncidium with thick dark leaves and a flower stalk 5 ft. long. Flowers are yellow, spotted with brown. Now quite rare.

Mule Ear Orchid

Cigar Orchid

LEATHER FERN is the largest fern in the U.S.—growing to 12 ft. high in the Everglades and Keys. Leaves thick; stalks hairy. There are over a hundred species of ferns in Florida. Over half are found in Everglades.

STRAP FERN grows on dead trees and humus in hammocks. Four species of this tropical group are found in and near the Park.

LADDER BRAKE, common in drier parts of the Park and Keys, is a close relative of the more northern species of bracken.

GRASS or SHOESTRING FERN often grows on trunks of palmetto as an epiphyte (p. 60). Leaves 16-20 in. long are grass-like.

RESURRECTION FERN, a polypody, grows on trees. Dries up in unfavorable weather; unrolls and grows after rains.

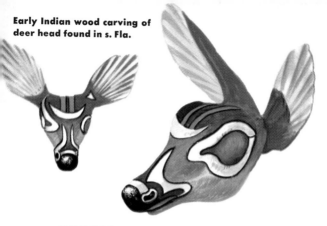

Early Indian wood carving of deer head found in s. Fla.

PEOPLE AND THIS LAND

The Everglades and the Keys may have been inhabited for many thousands of years, but proof of habitation goes back only three thousand years at the most. The record, though clear, is scanty and we know very little about the first Indians of this region, though Europeans were in contact with them for over two centuries.

The Calusa Indians inhabited this area at the time the first Spaniards arrived. This powerful tribe controlled the region south of Tampa, including the Everglades and Keys. Their influence extended north along the Atlantic coast to Cape Canaveral.

The Calusa lived in small bands of twenty to thirty, hunting, fishing, gathering wild plants, and doing a bit of agriculture. They were expert seamen, often traveling as far as Cuba in their small, open canoes. For war, or for religious occasions, the small bands joined together. They probably joined, also, in building the canals and large mounds, remains of which can still be seen in the Everglades National Park.

Calusa Indian watching wreck of Spanish ship

From the time the first Spanish vessels ran aground in the Keys about 1500, the Calusa were on hand to kill the crews and make off with plunder. A fleet of 80 Calusa canoes attacked Ponce de Leon in 1513. Later he was wounded by them and died in Cuba. In 1567 the Spanish established missions in Calusa territory, and under the Spanish influence the Indians confined their plundering to French and British vessels. In the long run, this choice of allies worked against the Calusa. The British and their Creek Indian allies (later known as Seminoles and Micco-sukees) pushed south and forced the Calusa from their land. At their height the Calusa numbered about 3,000 people in over 60 villages. But, as they were pushed into the Everglades, the Calusa gave up these settlements in favor of smaller camps. When Spain ceded Florida to Great Britain in 1763, a group of "Calusas," and other coastal Indians moved to Havana. The few Calusa left lived in the Everglades and on the Keys. Not much is known of them. They may have formed the group later known as the Spanish or Muspa Indians. Perhaps this group was mainly Seminole. At any rate, these Spanish Indians attacked American troops in 1839, and in 1840 killed Dr. Henry Perrine, the great agriculturist, on Indian Key. At this time the band numbered about a hundred, and soon they disappeared completely.

TEKESTA were a smaller tribe living around Miami and southward into the upper Keys. This small tribe was closely related to the Calusa, and like them, kept an unquiet peace with the Spanish. A Tekesta mission was established, destroyed, and rebuilt again. During the period from 1650 to 1750 the Indians gradually lost ground and died off. The group of "Calusa" which went to Cuba in 1763 were largely Tekesta Indians and members of the Ais tribe, who lived along Indian River to the north. No Calusa or Tekesta are alive today. They have been replaced by the Seminoles and Miccosukees.

bowl

shell digging tool

bone needles

beads

whetstone

sinker

Calusa relics found in southwest Florida

Indian chickee north of Tamiami Trail

For many years all Florida Indians have been incorrectly called Seminoles. There are actually two separate tribes, the Seminoles and the Miccosukees. Both groups have a similar language with slightly different dialects. They were originally Creek Indians from Georgia, who began to move southward about 1715, entering what is now Florida about 1750. By 1767 there was a settlement near Tampa Bay, and during the next decade migration increased. It reached its peak after the Creek War in 1813.

Villages were originally established in north and central Florida. Their population rose until it was close to 5,000. Each village supported itself with simple agriculture. Corn, squash, sweet potatoes, melons, and cowpeas were grown. Wild fruits and vegetables such as coco-plums, wild grapes, pond apples, and coontie rounded out their diet. Hunting supplied deer, turkey, and much small game. Game also furnished skins for moccasins and robes. Some tools, implements, and ornaments were made of bone and wood, and they traded for metal tools and implements.

The Seminoles and Miccosukees did not enjoy Florida for long. Pressure from settlers and political entanglements got them involved in border fights and raids. Their acceptance of runaway slaves added to their troubles. Andrew Jackson led American forces against the Indians in 1817, and a longer, more bitter war was fought from 1835 to 1842. In this war, about 1,500 Americans were killed. Osceola and other chiefs were captured by treachery; villages were burned, and most of the Seminoles and Miccosukees were moved to Indian territory (Oklahoma). Those that remained fled south into the cypress swamps and Everglades, and for a time carried on guerilla warfare against their enemies.

In all, about 500 Indians remained in Florida. These learned how to live in the wet wilderness. They developed the chickee as a shelter, and modified their simple agriculture. Fishing became more important and canoe building arose as a fine craft. Cotton clothing was obtained by barter, and with the advent of the sewing machine, about 1890, the bright multi-colored costumes were developed. These costumes are still very much a part of their culture today.

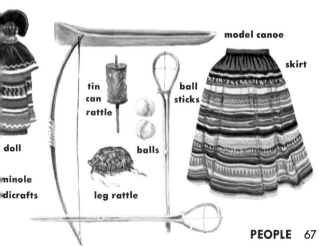

doll

minole
dicrafts

tin
can
rattle

balls

leg rattle

model canoe

ball
sticks

skirt

The Indian population increased slowly at first, but more rapidly during the past twenty years. Now there are over a thousand Seminoles and Miccosukees in Florida. Most of them live on the large reservations at Brighton, Big Cypress, and Dania, but there are several Miccosukee villages along the Tamiami Trail.

Young Indians attend local or Indian schools. Job opportunities are limited, and most men work in rural occupations. The women make craftwork to sell. They are best noted for their intricate sewing. Small pieces of brightly colored cloth are sewed into strips of geometric designs. These are combined in making skirts, blouses, and smaller articles. Dolls made of saw-palmetto fiber are also made and sold.

Visit the Miccosukees and Seminoles along the Tamiami Trail and on the reservations. Remember you are their guests. They were never conquered.

SPANIARDS probably touched south Florida in the early 1500's. When Ponce de León arrived in 1513, the Calusa already had gold and silver from Spanish shipwrecks. De León, Miruelo, Cordova, De Soto, and other explorers did not fare well with the Indians. When Ponce de León returned in 1521 he was fatally wounded by the Calusa. Soon Florida became a base for forts to protect the Spanish galleons en route from Mexico to Spain. With the soldiers came priests who also made little headway with the Indians. The early history of Florida is one of murder, treachery and reprisal, with short periods of unstable peace.

In northern Florida the Spanish missions were more successful, but these were destroyed by the British (1702-1704). Florida proved of such little value to Spain that, when the English conquered Havana, Spain traded all of Florida for its return. And, in 1783, England in turn swapped it back to Spain for the Bahamas.

During all this time the Keys, called Los Martires (the martyrs) by the Spanish, kept taking their toll of ships

Coins from shipwrecks on Florida Keys

and men as winds threw the heavy cargo vessels against the shoals and reefs. First the Indians and then the settlers took to plundering and later to salvaging wrecks. For fifty years before the United States acquired Florida, and for some years after, piracy was a hazard of the region. Sailing ships of all nations were captured by marauders with bases in the Keys, the Bahamas, and Caribbean islands. The most famous Florida pirate was Jose Gaspar, who sailed from Charlotte Harbor near Fort Myers until 1820, when the United States, Britain and Spain united against the pirates and captured about 100 ships and 1,700 men.

With a new naval base at Key West, the Keys began to grow. They became the center for wreckers and salvage crews who came when the area was cleared of pirates, and who stayed until lighthouses were built 30 years later.

Shrimp boats at Key West

Pineapple and coconut plantations were set out and attempts were made to introduce tropical plants. Dr. Henry Perrine brought agave and other plants from Mexico and set out nurseries in the Keys. He worked unceasingly through the early 1800's, only to be killed during an Indian raid in 1840.

About this same time, in 1832, John James Audubon came to the Keys. He set up headquarters at Key West, explored, sketched, paint-

Audubon painted the White-crowned Pigeon on the Keys.

ed, and collected bird skins. He kept detailed notes, not only about birds but about the land and events—even to the account of a hurricane. Audubon moved up to Indian Key, from which he explored Florida Bay and Cape Sable before continuing his journeys.

As the growth of this region continued, Fort Jefferson was begun on the Dry Tortugas in 1846, and two other forts at Key West. These soon became obsolete, and one was never finished. Fort Jefferson housed prisoners during the Civil War, including Dr. Samuel Mudd, who set Booth's broken leg after the actor assassinated Lincoln.

In the early 1900's, with railroads established, commercial fishing and raising of winter vegetables were started in south Florida. Everglades land was cleared, drainage canals were dug, and fishing camps sprang up in the Keys and along Florida Bay. But this industry was marginal at best, and earning a living was hard.

One industry which began in the 1870's, and grew rapidly, was plume-hunting. Egrets and herons had long been killed for food by Indians and settlers. Now fashion demanded the fine egret plumes, which the birds developed only during the nesting season. Hunters turned professional in the Everglades and on the Keys. The huge rookeries of nesting birds were easy targets, and thousands upon thousands of skins and feathers were exported for the millinery trade.

By 1900 the flocks were so badly depleted that the Audubon Society, in cooperation with the State of Florida, provided wardens to protect the nesting sites. Scarcity of plumes and higher prices only spurred poaching, and in protecting the birds, two wardens were killed. The death of one, Guy Bradley, was widely publicized, and eventually legislation, first in New York and then nationally, brought all plume-hunting to an end. The depleted flocks have gradually come back, but not in the great numbers of the past. There are still problems of food, water and control of the environment to be solved for these birds.

Plume hunters once killed thousands of breeding egrets.

U.S. 1 connects the Florida Keys.

Improved transportation opened up the isolated Everglades and the Keys. Until the railroad reached Miami in 1896, this was frontier country. Soon after, plans to push the railroad south to Key West were under way, and the actual work began in 1905. Seven years and twenty million dollars later the job was done.

The railroad bucked hurricanes during construction and after. Finally, after 23 years, the great hurricane of 1935 finished it off. Meanwhile, the trip across south Florida was a ten-day adventure. The much-heralded Tamiami Trail (Tampa to Miami) was begun in 1916 as a county project. In 1924 the state took over and by 1928 the road was done. It has been constantly improved, and will eventually be four-laned. Trip time now—four hours.

A road down the Keys had been started in 1923. It eventually made Key West with the aid of 40 miles of ferry. After the 1935 hurricane, three years were spent in converting the wrecked railroad bed into a modern highway. When completed, it linked 29 islands by bridges and fills that covered 37 miles of water. The longest bridge is 7 miles in length; the highest is 65 feet above the sea. So engineering skill and hard work opened this tropical area for residents and visitors.

Marina at Flamingo in the Park

THE PARK STORY has many roots. Famous visitors, impressed by the great rookeries and the lush plant life of the Everglades hammocks, spread the story. Steps taken to save the rookeries paved the way for wider conservation efforts. In 1915 the Florida Federation of Women's Clubs obtained 960 acres to preserve a fine hammock of royal palms. The state added 4,000 acres in 1921, making the area Royal Palm State Park.

About this time the idea of creating a national park in the Everglades began to take hold. Individuals and organizations pushed the idea until the Florida legislature started the project in 1929. The next year hearings were held, and Congress designated the area as a proposed park in 1934. Acquisition of land moved slowly during World War II, but men like Ernest Coe, John Baker, and John Pennekamp, with a Park Commission of 25 men, kept the project moving. Finally enough marginal, private, and state land was obtained to meet the minimum park requirements. In 1947 President Truman dedicated the new Everglades National Park.

The Everglades National Park encompasses about one and a half million acres—nearly twice the size of the state of Rhode Island. See pp. 4-5 for a detailed map. Only two other national parks are larger—Denali in Alaska and Yellowstone in Wyoming. Nearly every plant and animal described in this Guide can be found within the Park limits, and many more as well. Records show the presence of approximately 300 kinds of birds, 30 kinds of mammals, 65 kinds of reptiles and amphibians, 300 fishes, and almost a thousand species of flowering plants.

Daniel B. Beard, the Park's first Superintendent, worked for ten years to preserve this rich area and to develop the Park facilities. The task continues. Threats to the Park's wildlife include changes in water flow and nutrient pollution. A project to restore the quality and quantity of water entering Everglades National Park has begun. Park boundaries have been expanded to include vital marsh habitat. Although species recovery is slow, more than a million visitors a year enjoy Everglades National Park.

Lectures are given by rangers.

STOP AND LOOK The Park is not a place where you can hurry through from one quick sight to another. Neither can you see it as you go along the road, though the broad vistas of sea, grass and sky are impressive. To see the Park, stop frequently. Take time to look. Wait quietly at the edge of a slough or at one of the wayside stations. Soon you will be seeing the many creatures from alligators to zebra butter-flies that make the Park the gem that it is.

ROYAL PALM STATION AND EXHIBITS is reached on a branch from the Flamingo road. Watch for the sign. Visit the wildlife exhibits. Watch fish, alligators, turtles, and many birds in a nearby slough.

ANHINGA TRAIL, a short distance from the Royal Palm station, is an elevated walk over a slough, taking you right into the wet Ever-glades. Bring your field glasses and camera. Stay awhile to look for anhingas and gallinules, alligators, water snakes and gars.

GUMBO-LIMBO TRAIL is also near the Royal Palm station. This marked and labeled nature trail takes you through a rich hammock.

DRIVE TO FLAMINGO along the 38-mile road gives you views of the Everglades, hammocks and mangroves. Stop along the way at road-side stations. Read the signs; watch for wildlife.

MAHOGANY HAMMOCK is one of several turnoffs. See the largest mahogany trees in the U.S. From Pa-hay-okee Overlook view sawgrass country or follow the Mangrove Trail at West Lake. Stay overnight at Long Pine Key campground and take the Pinelands Trail.

FLAMINGO was once an old fishing settlement. Visit the exhibits and public buildings. Here are restaurants, overnight accommodations, camping and picnicking. Watch water birds from the Eco Pond raised viewing platform or along the Florida Bay shore.

BOAT TRIPS depart from Flamingo and Everglades City. These are educational, safe, guided tours.

EXPLORE the Everglades on foot near Flamingo, and on the trails. Get proper equipment and advice before venturing back-country. Explore by rented boat at Flamingo, but stay on marked routes. Use a chart. Get a guide to go farther afield.

FISH in the many canals, rivers and lakes of the Everglades. Florida Bay is excellent too. The park maintains free boat launching ramps at Flamingo. A fishing license is required throughout the park.

PHOTOGRAPH the great sweep of the Everglades or the majestic flight of birds. Catch a sleeping alligator or a gallinule picking its way across the water lilies. A telephoto lens pays off here.

WALKS AND TALKS with Park rangers are a feature during most of the year at Flamingo, Royal Palm and Everglades City. Check bulletin boards in the Park for details, or ask at Park Headquarters.

BISCAYNE NATIONAL PARK consists of 181,500 acres of pristine waters, subtropical islands and living coral reefs. The park includes the northernmost islands of the Florida Keys, southern Biscayne Bay and coral patch reefs. The mainland and island shorelines are fringed with protective stands of mangrove trees that provide vital nutrients to marine life. This is a park with spectacular underwater scenery and offers opportunities for snorkeling, scuba diving, sailing, water skiing, swimming, and fishing. Explore coral reefs, shipwrecks, mangrove channels and productive grassbeds. Park headquarters is located on Convoy Point (see map, p. 5) nine miles east of Homestead, Florida. Follow U.S. 1 south and turn left on N. Canal Drive (S.W. 328th St.). Information is available at park headquarters. Write to P.O. Box 1369, Homestead FL 33090-1369 or phone (305) 247-7275 (PARK).

BIG CYPRESS NATIONAL PRESERVE consists of 720,000 acres, or about 50% of the total area of the Big Cypress Swamp (see map, p. 5). The threat posed to the watershed of Everglades National Park caused Congress to establish this preserve in 1974. The 1980s brought more enlightened attitudes toward watersheds and wetlands, and today Florida is much involved in environmental protection efforts. Now we are back simply trying nature's way while allowing for recreational enjoyment. Two major highways cross the preserve, Alligator Alley (I-75) and Tamiami Trail (U.S. 41). With Rt. 29 to the west, they enable you to explore the Big Cypress. For information write to S. R. Box 110, Ochopee, FL 33943, or visit the headquarters at Ochopee or the Oasis Vistor Center on U.S. 41.

HOMESTEAD BAYFRONT PARK is a county park located on Biscayne Bay adjacent to Biscayne National Park about nine miles east of Homestead. There is an entry fee; swimming, boating, fishing, and picnicking are allowed. Boat ramp available.

REDLANDS is the famed agricultural region near Homestead and Florida City. It can be easily seen when visiting either the Park or Keys. Drive east or west from Homestead through fields of tomatoes, beans, squash, and other winter vegetables. Groves of avocados, mangos, limes, and papaya can be seen.

WHAT TO DO AND SEE IN THE AREA

DRIVE DOWN THE KEYS on U. S. 1. Going south from Key Largo junction, it is approximately 110 miles to Key West over fill and bridges. You can stop at many places in between. There are ample accommodations, restaurants, fishing, swimming, and commercial attractions along the way. Key West is the southernmost city in continental U. S. Many of its inhabitants choose to be called "conchs" (pronounced conks), a name given to settlers of the 1800's, a mixture of Bahamians, Cubans, English, and Americans who plied their trades as fishermen, marine salvagers, and merchants. Many of the old conch houses built in the 1800's still stand in this picturesque area. One of the famous landmarks is Hemingway Home, now a state museum, built in 1851; another is Audubon House, where wildlife artist John James Audubon created his famous paintings of birds of the Keys.

MORE INFORMATION

VISIT THE EVERGLADES WEBSITE at http://www.nps.gov/ever

JOIN ORGANIZATIONS interested in natural history and conservation of this region. Learn from them and support them. Among such organizations are:

FLORIDA NATIONAL PARKS AND MONUMENTS ASSOCIATION, 10 Parachute Key #51, Homestead, FL 33034, furthers the understanding of the natural historic values of the Everglades National Park, Biscayne National Park, Big Cypress National Reserve and Dry Tortugas National Park. This non-profit organization operates park visitor center bookstores where literature and other items can be purchased that assist the visiting public in better understanding these unique natural areas. Proceeds from sales are used to support visitor-related park programs.
Phone: 305-247-1216
Fax: 305-247-1225

INDEX

Asterisks (*) denote pages on which the subjects are illustrated.

MEASURING SCALE (IN 10THS OF AN INCH)